THE BOYS' GUIDE TO GROWING UP

Phil Wilkinson

Illustrated by Sarah Horne

Contents

WHAT IS PUBERTY?

In the next few years, you will start to notice some pretty big changes happening to your body – both on the outside and the inside!

These changes will affect how you look, feel and even think. It might sound scary, but the more you know about puberty, the more you'll be able to handle these new changes.

Puberty is the name given to the normal process that turns your body from a boy's into a man's. It means that as you grow up, you'll slowly get taller, heavier and more muscular. Your voice will change, and you'll get more hair on your body.

The purpose of puberty isn't just to turn you into an adult man. It's to get your body ready in case you want to have children one day.

The most important thing to remember is that there's no need to be embarrassed; puberty is normal and natural.

YOUR PUBERTY TIMELINE

Your body has its own unique internal clock, and it will only start puberty when it's ready. However, this is a rough guide to what will happen to your body and when.

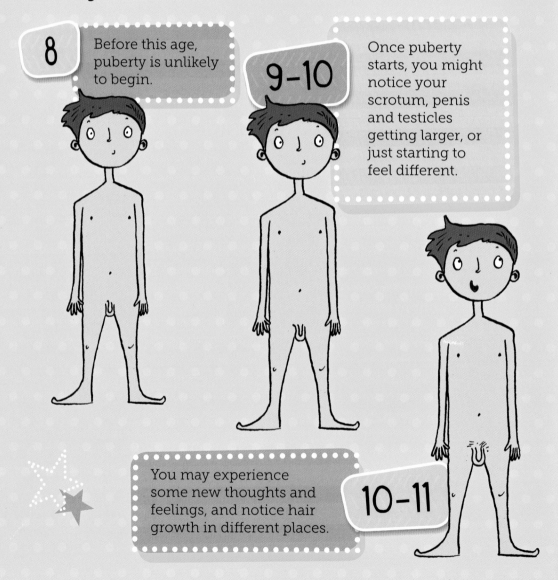

8 Before this age, puberty is unlikely to begin.

9-10 Once puberty starts, you might notice your scrotum, penis and testicles getting larger, or just starting to feel different.

You may experience some new thoughts and feelings, and notice hair growth in different places.

10-11

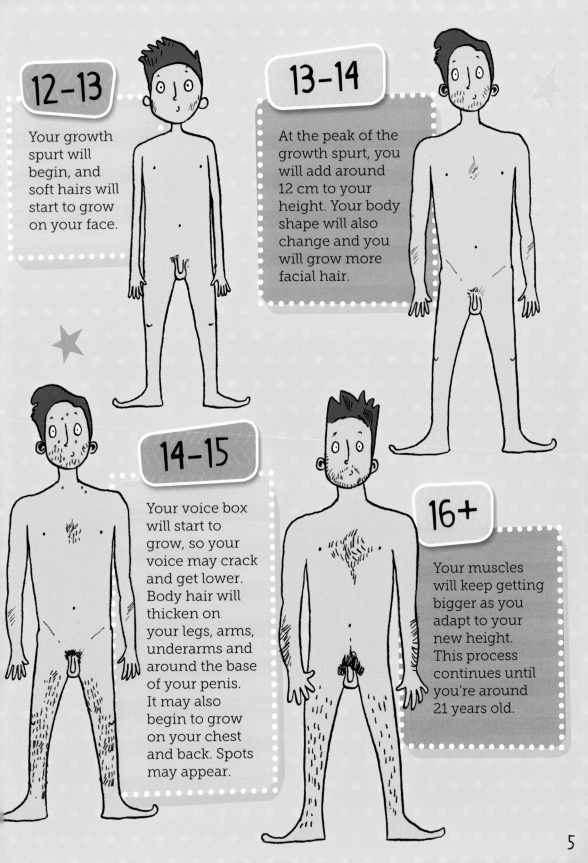

12-13

Your growth spurt will begin, and soft hairs will start to grow on your face.

13-14

At the peak of the growth spurt, you will add around 12 cm to your height. Your body shape will also change and you will grow more facial hair.

14-15

Your voice box will start to grow, so your voice may crack and get lower. Body hair will thicken on your legs, arms, underarms and around the base of your penis. It may also begin to grow on your chest and back. Spots may appear.

16+

Your muscles will keep getting bigger as you adapt to your new height. This process continues until you're around 21 years old.

5

HOW DO HORMONES WORK?

**Everyone experiences puberty in different ways,
but it all starts in your brain.**

Hormones are like messengers that are carried around in your blood to make parts of your body change. At around the age of 10, your brain starts to make a hormone called GnRH. GnRH sends a signal to your testicles to start making male sex hormones known as androgens and testosterone. These sex hormones trigger the start of puberty, when the male sex cell, known as sperm, starts to be made in your testicles.

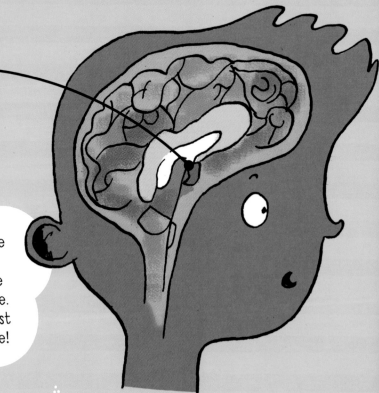

A part of the brain called the hypothalamus makes GnRH.

Boys have some female hormones, and girls have a bit of the male hormone testosterone. Sounds odd, but it's just the way we are made!

The sex hormones also kickstart all the other changes involved in puberty, which carry on until you are around 21 years old. These changes can be thrilling, and will make you feel more grown up.

Hormones can make you feel angry, frustrated and annoyed, and at other times extremely happy and wild with excitement. When they are charging around your body it can feel strange and unsettling, but don't worry; eventually your feelings will settle down.

THE HEIGHT AND WEIGHT RACE

You may think that you and your friends all look different now, but wait until you hit puberty!

Some of your friends will start to grow by 11, while others will remain looking the same until they are around 14 years old. It can be annoying if you are first or last, but don't worry – it's not a race and you can handle it.

Puberty doesn't happen neatly. That means your body won't grow in an equal and logical way. Some boys will find they put on weight first. Others will find that their height shoots upwards, while some will notice their feet growing first.

What to expect

- ★ Boys get taller and heavier. Your height will increase by about 12 cm during puberty.

- ★ Your muscles will get bigger.

- ★ Boys' upper bodies start to look different to girls'. Your shoulders will broaden as your muscles develop.

You may also experience growing pains. These are dull, achy pains that happen around the age of 12 and affect your arms, legs and even back. They are normal, but see your doctor if they start to get you down.

Am I getting breasts?

Almost half of all boys notice some breast swelling at puberty. Don't worry – they won't be like female breasts! The swelling happens as a reaction to the surges of hormones. It goes down, but do talk to your doctor if it's bothering you.

A DEEPER VOICE

Open your mouth to speak during puberty and another change becomes very obvious!

Changes to your voice generally start to happen when you are around 14 years old, but, like all of puberty, they could start a little earlier or later. Your voice will become lower, deeper and more grown-up, a process known as your voice 'breaking'.

FACTS ABOUT VOCAL CHANGES

★ Vocal cords are the thin muscles that stretch across your larynx like rubber bands. When you speak, the cords vibrate, creating the sound of your voice.

★ Before puberty, the vocal cords are small. During puberty they get much larger, which makes your voice sound deeper.

★ Your face grows during puberty. As your facial bones get bigger, spaces are created in the nose and throat, which makes your voice louder.

Vocal cord

Larynx

Your voice doesn't *actually* break, of course, and the change isn't always a quick one. This is because your vocal cords need to adjust as the larynx gets bigger. Sometimes your voice will be normal, other times it will be wobbly and squeaky, and sometimes it will sound grown-up.

Dealing with voice wobbles is easy! Cough, clear your throat and try again, or swallow and wait a few seconds before you speak.

Wha—!

What's with the lump in my throat?

This lump, called an Adam's apple, is not a new part of your body. It's simply your larger larynx tilting at a different angle in the throat, which makes it stick out a little as you get older.

SPOTTY SKIN

You might be dreading spots – but when you know what they are and how to deal with them, you'll feel much more prepared.

Zits, pimples, blackheads ... whatever you call them, spots can be a pain when you're growing up. But taking good care of your skin is an important part of going through puberty.

Spots are triggered by the male sex hormones known as androgens. These hormones control the making of a special oil in the skin called sebum. Usually just enough sebum is made to keep the skin smooth. However, at puberty, androgens surge around your body. This makes oil glands produce too much sebum, which then blocks tiny holes in your skin called pores. Once a pore is blocked, a spot is formed: either a blackhead, which happens when the oil solidifies under the skin; or a red swelling, which happens when the oil mixes with bacteria.

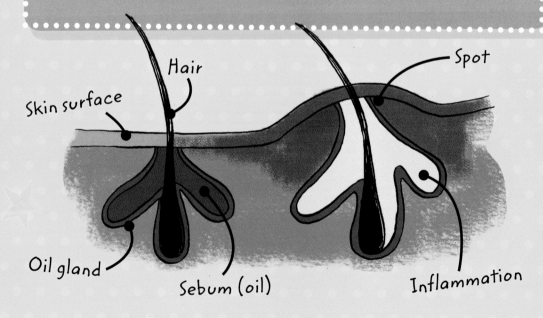

Hair

Spot

Skin surface

Oil gland

Sebum (oil)

Inflammation

The good news is you don't have to suffer through spots silently. There are loads of spot treatments that can help. Most can be bought from chemists, or doctors can offer stronger treatment on prescription for more serious outbreaks, known as acne.

Why is my back spotty?

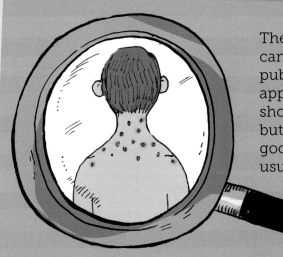

The male hormone testosterone can make spots worse during puberty. On boys, spots tend to appear on the neck, upper back, shoulders and chest. It's annoying but perfectly normal, and with a good skincare routine you can usually manage them.

HAIR, HAIR, EVERYWHERE

Hair in new places is one of the most surprising parts of puberty.

Where once your skin was smooth, soon you'll start to see hair slowly sprouting up. It's often the first sign of puberty that you'll notice, and can appear from when you are 9 years old, although you will probably be a bit older.

Hair will grow across the pubic region around your penis, and may grow up towards your lower belly. It will also start to grow under your arms, on your chest and possibly on your shoulders and back too. The hair on your legs and arms will also change; during puberty it gets thicker and darker, and you'll start to see more of it appearing.

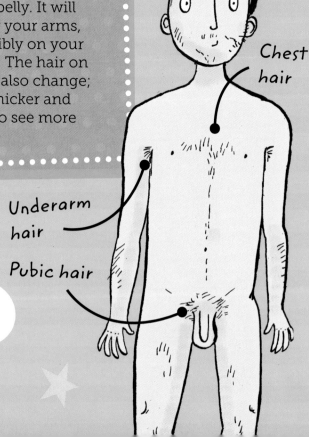

Chest hair

Underarm hair

Pubic hair

You can't control how much hair you will grow – it just depends on how your body is made.

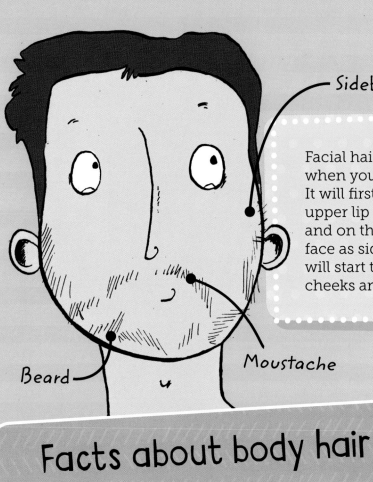

Sideburns

Facial hair starts to grow when you are about 12 or 13. It will first appear on your upper lip as a moustache, and on the sides of your face as sideburns. Then it will start to grow on your cheeks and chin.

Beard

Moustache

Facts about body hair

★ Body hair, especially pubic hair, can be a different colour to the hair on your head. Some boys find their facial hair is a different colour to their head hair too.

★ Body hair doesn't get long in the way the hair on your head does.

★ How dark and thick your hair is depends on your ethnic background: where your family is from.

THE ART OF SHAVING

Facial hair has a soft, wispy look to it when it first appears. Some boys find it grows in patches, while others get a full beard quite quickly.

Whether you decide to start shaving and when is up to you. Some boys don't mind the patchy hair and are quite happy to leave it growing for a few years. Others want to grow a beard, while some don't like the look of facial hair and prefer to shave it off completely.

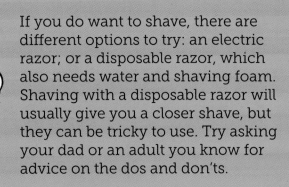

If you do want to shave, there are different options to try: an electric razor; or a disposable razor, which also needs water and shaving foam. Shaving with a disposable razor will usually give you a closer shave, but they can be tricky to use. Try asking your dad or an adult you know for advice on the dos and don'ts.

It's very common to get nicks and cuts when you start shaving. If this happens, make sure you wash the area with water and then press cotton wool against it to stop the bleeding. Check out the back of the book for where to get more shaving advice.

When you start shaving, your hair grows back as stubble. For your face to stay smooth, you'll need to shave the stubble off. At first the regrowth might take a whole week, but eventually you'll need to shave about once a day.

Will shaving make my spots worse?

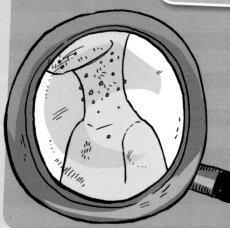

Shaving can make the skin sore and encourage spots to appear. The best way to shave if you have spots is to use an electric razor or a safety razor. Avoid multi-blade razors, which can make the skin very irritated.

SWEAT, SMELLS AND PERSONAL HYGIENE

If you know how to handle smells, it'll be no sweat!

Puberty can be a sweaty time. You may find you sweat when you're nervous, embarrassed, walking about and even when you're sleeping.

There's nothing wrong with sweat – your body needs it to cool down. However, it will begin to smell when it mixes with bacteria lurking on your skin. If you don't wash, you'll get what's known as body odour (BO for short).

The best way to control BO is to shower daily with soap, use an antiperspirant deodorant to help control how much you sweat, and wear clean clothes and underwear every day.

Some boys suffer from extreme sweat at puberty and no normal antiperspirant will help. If you find that is the case for you, don't worry. There are stronger antiperspirants that your doctor can prescribe.

What's with the smell down below?

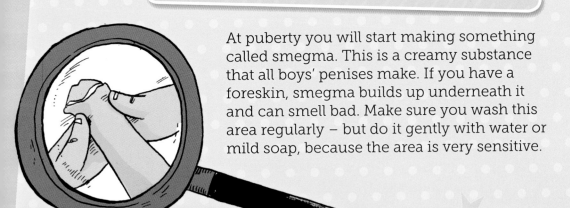

At puberty you will start making something called smegma. This is a creamy substance that all boys' penises make. If you have a foreskin, smegma builds up underneath it and can smell bad. Make sure you wash this area regularly — but do it gently with water or mild soap, because the area is very sensitive.

CHANGES DOWN BELOW

Throughout puberty you'll see big, but gradual, changes happening between your legs.

Your sex organs will grow and mature from the start of puberty. This will allow you to start producing sperm, so that one day you'll be able to make babies if you want to.

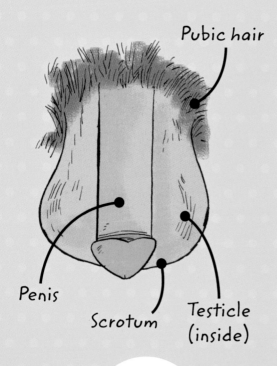

Pubic hair

Penis

Scrotum

Testicle (inside)

Scrotum

Your scrotum, which holds your testicles, will start to get bigger and longer, and will darken in colour. You'll also find that the skin of your scrotum will get looser and baggier, and that the scrotum will hang lower. This is because your body is too warm for sperm, the male sex cell produced in the testicles. However, when you're cold, your scrotum will get smaller to pull your testicles nearer to your body's warmth.

There are lots of silly names for our private parts. Testicles are sometimes called balls, nuts, gonads and even the family jewels!

Testicles inside your scrotum

Once your brain sends the puberty messages to your testicles, they will start to change and grow. When they reach a certain size they will start to produce sperm. Sperm are only designed to live for a few days, so your testicles keep making new ones all the time.

Pubic hair

Pubic hair will start to grow around the base of your penis, in the area known as the genital or pubic region. The hair will spread towards your thighs and might creep up towards your tummy. It starts off very soft, and later becomes curlier and darker.

Why does one testicle hang lower than the other?

It's very normal for one testicle (usually the left) to hang lower than the other. This stops them hitting each other when you're running about.

MORE CHANGES DOWN BELOW

Your penis will also start to change during puberty, both in appearance and behaviour!

Like everything to do with puberty, the changes that happen to your penis will depend on your own body, so they may or may not be the same as what happens to your friends' penises.

Semen

About a year after your testicles grow, you may have what's known as an 'ejaculation' from your penis. This happens when you become sexually excited and your penis becomes hard, or erect. As you get more excited, you'll feel muscle movements in your penis – these will squirt out a sticky fluid mixed with sperm, known as semen. This process is called ejaculating, or coming.

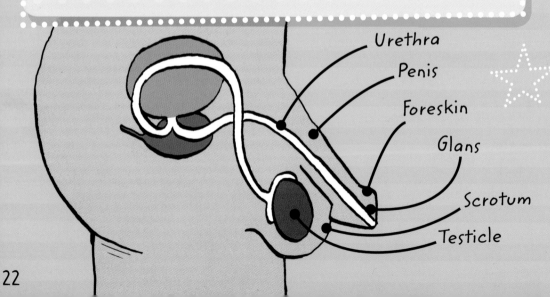

Urethra

Penis

Foreskin

Glans

Scrotum

Testicle

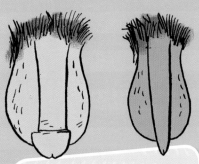 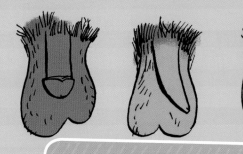

Foreskin

This is the skin that covers the end of your penis. It protects the head of the penis, or glans, and will get bigger during puberty.

All boys are born with a foreskin, but sometimes it is removed, or circumcised, for religious or medical reasons. Whether you have been circumcised makes no difference to hygiene.

Getting bigger

Testosterone from the testicles will make your penis grow in length and width. It won't grow very much in length, but it will increase in girth. The glans will also get bigger.

Many boys become anxious about the size of their penis, but don't worry. The size of your penis when it's soft and floppy is different to when it's erect – and size doesn't affect how it works.

What's with the bumps on my penis?

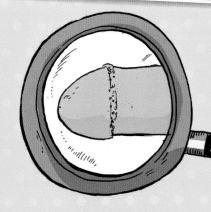

One boy in every three will have bumps on his penis, known as penile papules. These are harmless and hardly noticeable to others, so don't worry about them.

NEW FEELINGS

Some of the changes that puberty brings are exciting and fun to see, but there are also some that may startle you a bit.

You may start thinking about sex a lot more during puberty – this is perfectly normal, and nothing to worry about.

Sexual feelings

Some boys find that they start becoming attracted to people they never thought about before: perhaps a girl who lives nearby, or a boy they admire. If this happens to you, you might start imagining kissing or touching them. This is a safe way of exploring your new feelings, but don't let anyone pressure you into dating or kissing someone before you're ready. You might also find that you are not attracted to anyone. This is normal too, and you shouldn't feel worried about it.

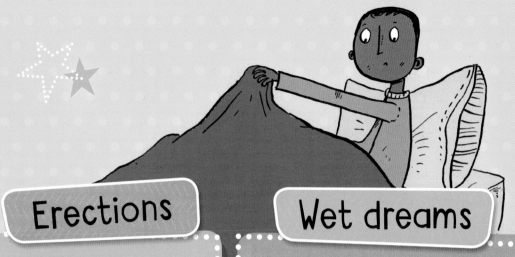

Erections

You will already have had some erections, since they begin at a very early age. However, during puberty erections become much more frequent. Many are caused by new sexual feelings or something exciting, but some happen for no reason at all.

Wet dreams

A wet dream is when you ejaculate in your sleep. It's the result of a dream about sex, which you might remember or might not. Wet dreams are very common, and are nothing to be ashamed about. They stop when you get older, but in the meantime, just wipe off the semen, have a shower and throw your sheets and PJs in the washing machine.

Why am I getting erections out of the blue?

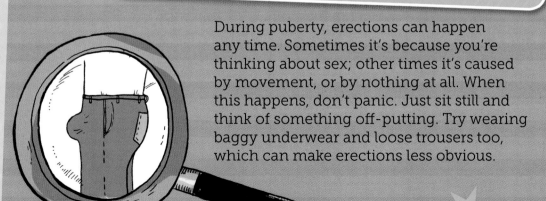

During puberty, erections can happen any time. Sometimes it's because you're thinking about sex; other times it's caused by movement, or by nothing at all. When this happens, don't panic. Just sit still and think of something off-putting. Try wearing baggy underwear and loose trousers too, which can make erections less obvious.

SEX EXPLAINED

Puberty means your body is preparing to have babies one day. This will be your choice, but your body gets ready anyway.

Despite what your body is planning, having babies is probably the furthest thing from your mind right now! Even so, it is important to know what sex is and how babies are made, so that you can understand why your body is doing new things.

Lots of people find the whole topic of sex very embarrassing to discuss or even say, but sex is a normal activity between adult people who love and care about each other.

What's sex?

During sex, two people kiss, cuddle and get sexually excited. When a man is excited, his penis gets hard, also known as erect. When a woman is excited, her vagina releases a slippery fluid. The vagina is a passage that starts between a woman's legs and goes into her body.

When a man and a woman have sex, the man's penis goes inside the woman's vagina. When the man reaches the peak of excitement, he ejaculates and a small amount of semen is released. Semen contains millions of sperm that swim into the woman's body and try to reach an egg.

Sex isn't just about making babies. It's also something adults do when they love each other, because it's a way for them to show affection and to feel good. See the next page for how people can choose to have sex without making babies.

What's with this gross sex stuff?

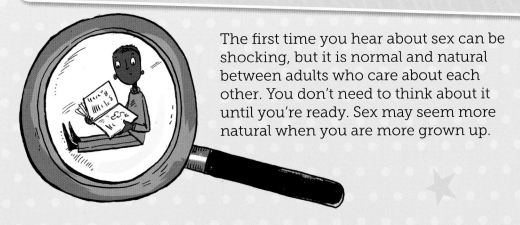

The first time you hear about sex can be shocking, but it is normal and natural between adults who care about each other. You don't need to think about it until you're ready. Sex may seem more natural when you are more grown up.

MAKING BABIES

To make a baby, sperm from a man's body has to meet and join with a woman's egg.

Making a baby may seem very mysterious, but it is important to understand what your body can do.

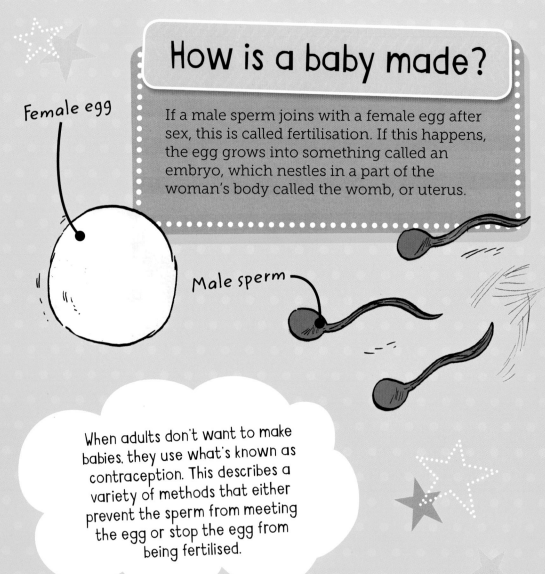

How is a baby made?

If a male sperm joins with a female egg after sex, this is called fertilisation. If this happens, the egg grows into something called an embryo, which nestles in a part of the woman's body called the womb, or uterus.

Female egg

Male sperm

When adults don't want to make babies, they use what's known as contraception. This describes a variety of methods that either prevent the sperm from meeting the egg or stop the egg from being fertilised.

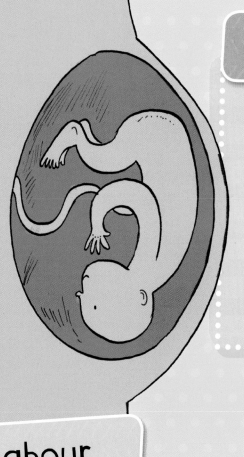

Pregnancy

Pregnancy is the time a baby develops inside the mother. A pregnancy lasts nine months, in which the embryo develops into a baby. The growing child stretches the uterus, which is why a bump appears when a woman is pregnant.

Labour

The process of giving birth is known as labour. A baby can arrive by vaginal delivery, where the woman pushes the baby out through her vagina, or by a method called a caesarean section, when doctors open the woman's uterus in surgery to get the baby out.

KEEPING YOUR CONFIDENCE UP

Having 'self-esteem', or confidence in your own abilities, can be challenging for both boys and girls.

How you feel about yourself and your body is an important part of puberty. You can help yourself to feel good!

The rapid changes of puberty can both boost your confidence and crush it, especially in the early years when your body is growing in ways that are surprising. Perhaps you feel you're too tall or too short, or too sweaty and smelly. Maybe your friends have grown big and muscly, while you still look like a kid.

One thing is almost guaranteed: you'll imagine things are much worse than they really are. Relax and let things happen at their own pace.

If you find yourself feeling low, try out these top tips:

★ Surround yourself with people you trust and like. Real friends don't make you feel bad for how you look, or push you to do things you don't want to do.

★ Don't compare yourself to others; it's guaranteed to make you feel bad about yourself.

★ Big yourself up. Sometimes faking confidence really does make you feel better.

★ Don't think you have to look like the men you see on TV and in films. The media likes to show body types that are very difficult to copy.

MOOD SWINGS

One of the biggest changes you'll notice at puberty is how you feel.

The hormones that are coursing around your body affect how you think, giving you really strong, intense emotions.

Your feelings will switch back and forth as your developing body is flooded with hormones. Sometimes you won't know how to handle them, but that's okay. During puberty you will learn to cope with intense emotions, particularly anger, just as it will take time to get to know your new body.

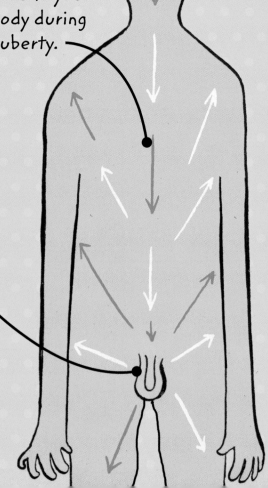

Brain

Hormones travel all around your body during puberty.

Testicles

Tiredness, stress and eating unhealthy foods can also affect your moods.

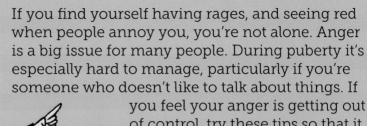

If you find yourself having rages, and seeing red when people annoy you, you're not alone. Anger is a big issue for many people. During puberty it's especially hard to manage, particularly if you're someone who doesn't like to talk about things. If you feel your anger is getting out of control, try these tips so that it doesn't get the better of you:

★ Learn to count to ten and walk away. This works every time, as it makes you breathe and calm down, and stops you from saying or doing something you'll regret.

★ Talk about it. This is a great way to manage your anger. Talking helps get to the root of the rage. Do you feel misunderstood, resentful or confused? Tell someone.

Can I just be by myself?

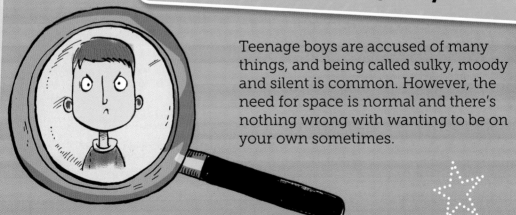

Teenage boys are accused of many things, and being called sulky, moody and silent is common. However, the need for space is normal and there's nothing wrong with wanting to be on your own sometimes.

MANAGING YOUR FEELINGS

Sometimes it can seem more acceptable for girls to talk about how they feel, and to sympathise with one other, than it is for boys.

That means it can be harder for boys to manage their feelings at puberty. This is true in some homes too, with mums talking and encouraging their daughters to talk, while dads and sons stay quiet. If that sounds familiar, there are some important things to know.

Talking helps

When you have bad and sad feelings, ignoring them doesn't work. Instead, all that happens is the feelings get worse. That's why talking to others is useful. If you can't talk to friends or family, look at the back of this book for places to go for help.

Just be yourself

You don't have to become the touchy-feely type to manage your feelings. Sometimes just saying, 'I feel awful', or, 'I can't control my anger' to an adult is enough.

Accept help from others

It can be hard to hear that you may need to work on your emotions, but advice from the right person can be a life-saver, especially if you feel scared or out of control.

Listen to your mates

Your friends are going through the same stuff as you. Try to read between the lines of what they are saying. If they joke a lot about their looks, they might be feeling sensitive. Try not to tease others, and ask them to stop if someone is teasing you.

Speak up if you're frightened

One of the pressures of being a boy can be feeling you have to be strong and brave all the time. If something scares you, whether it is your temper, someone else's behaviour or a situation, the brave thing to do is to speak up and tell someone.

HEALTHY EATING

Eating well during puberty is vital if you want to feel good. Healthy food will help you to have fewer mood swings and will allow your body to develop properly.

As you grow older, you can choose your own food more and more, especially when you're out and about. The urge to eat fast food or junk food can be strong.

If you want to look and feel healthy, you need to eat three main meals a day with fruit, vegetables and plenty of protein from meat, beans or eggs. This means you should limit food that has no nutritional value, like fizzy drinks, biscuits and crisps. You may be lucky enough to stay slim no matter what you eat, but eating junk food will still make you feel bloated and sluggish.

CRISPS

If you're worried about your weight, it can be tempting to go on a diet. This might put you on a rollercoaster of eating too little and then eating too much, which confuses your body. If you feel you need to lose or gain weight, ask your parents or your doctor for proper advice.

On average, boys put on about 17 kg during puberty. However, your height, diet and the genes you inherit from your parents will all influence how much weight you personally gain.

What's with my constant hunger?

Feed me!

To support the increase in your height and weight during puberty, you will need to eat more from about the age of 9 onwards. However, your appetite will increase even more at the time of your growth spurt around 13, and you may find that you're hungry all the time.

THE POWER OF EXERCISE

Exercise is good for your body and your mind. During your teenage years you need about 60 minutes of activity a day.

That much exercise may sound like a lot, but you might be doing more than you realise already.

Exercise can include everything from walking to school and taking the stairs to playing football with your mates. If you don't do anything active at the moment, you should get moving. If you don't like team sports, why not try martial arts, gymnastics or running? No matter what the exercise is, find something you love and do it at least three times a week.

As you get older you may notice pressure to achieve the muscular perfection of some male celebrities and models, which is why some boys hit the gym. However, boys grow muscles at different rates. Depending on your genes (the information inherited from your parents) and what you eat, you may be more or less muscular than your friends. So don't exercise too much to try and look like someone else; working out the wrong way can damage your growing body.

Why am I so tired?

The changes your body is going through, and the exercise your body needs to stay healthy, can make you very tired during puberty. Even though you might want to stay up late, you should be sleeping for 10 hours a night. This is important for proper growth and muscular development.

PRIVACY AND YOUR BODY

During puberty you'll start to feel the need for more privacy.

Part of growing up and becoming an independent person is choosing what you want to tell or show other people.

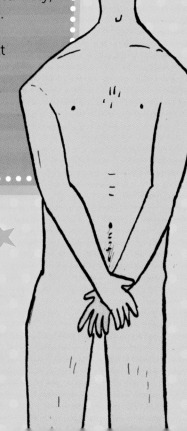

Needing privacy means you may not want to tell your parents everything you're thinking and feeling. You also may not want to spend as much time with them. This is normal behaviour. Talk to your parents and tell them what you need and why, so they can make life easier for you at home.

You may also start to feel that you don't want to get changed in front of others. This is your right, because your body is private. Then again, some boys don't mind being naked around their friends and family. It's really a case of what works for you.

Your genital area is private. No one should ask to see or touch your penis, or ask you to look at or touch anyone else's. There may be times, however, when you should show your parents or doctor if you have worries about your body.

It's hard enough to adjust to a new body shape without people being insensitive. You might need to remind people – especially your parents and siblings – that you are changing and don't always want someone in the bathroom when you're having a wash.

Get out!

Keeping your privates private doesn't mean your naked body is bad – there's no need to feel ashamed.

You might find that you and your friends start teasing each other about how you look. You may think these jokes are funny, or you may secretly hate the comments people make about your body. Be sensitive to others and speak out when you don't like the teasing.

PUBERTY FOR GIRLS

The girls you know are going through puberty too.

Like boys, the changes will affect every girl differently. Girls can begin puberty earlier, so some of the girls you know may be taller or look more grown-up than the boys.

Some of the changes girls go through are similar to yours: they get taller, heavier, grow body hair, get spots and develop their sex organs. However, they also grow breasts and start their periods, things that are a vital part of puberty for girls.

Like boys, girls go through puberty at different times and in different ways.

What are periods?

Also known as menstruation, periods are monthly bleeds that start when a girl's body is developed enough to have a baby one day. At this point, an egg from one of her ovaries will travel along the Fallopian tubes to her uterus each month.

To get ready for the egg, the uterus grows a thick lining made up of blood, tissue and fluid. Then, if the egg meets a sperm and is fertilised during sex, a baby can grow in the soft lining of the uterus. If the egg does not meet a sperm, then the lining is not needed. It breaks down naturally and leaves the girl's body through her vagina during her period.

Girls manage their periods by using products like tampons and sanitary pads that absorb the blood.

Uterus

Fallopian tube

Cervix

Ovary

Vagina

Tampon

Sanitary pad

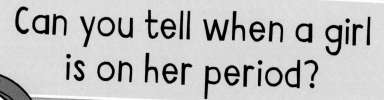

Can you tell when a girl is on her period?

No, you can't tell from the outside. It's a totally normal and healthy process – girls can do everything they usually do whilst on a period.

GIRLS HAVE WORRIES, TOO

Despite the physical differences, girls are just like you.

They also find puberty difficult, they have mood swings and they often worry about their growing bodies.

Girls have mood swings caused by hormones in the same way that boys do. However, for some girls these become worse around seven days before their periods, when something called premenstrual syndrome, or 'PMS' occurs. Premenstrual syndrome is the result of changing levels of hormones, and it leaves a lot of girls feeling low and tearful.

During their teenage years, girls may put on more fat than boys, who tend to put on more muscle. This may make them feel self-conscious and uncertain about their bodies at a time when they want to feel attractive.

Being teased, called names or having their growing parts pointed out will make girls insecure and upset. It's important to be kind during this stage of puberty.

If girls are being teased, you might think joining in will make you cool. It's actually a lot cooler to stand up for what is right, and to respect your friends.

How to be a boy who girls like

★ Don't make fun of how girls look

★ Don't crack jokes about periods or breasts

★ Be sympathetic if a girl you know is feeling low

★ Do stand up for someone who is being teased

★ Don't think girls won't understand what you're going through

Words to remember

acne   A skin condition that causes lots of spots.

androgens   Some of the male hormones that kickstart the whole puberty process.

body odour (BO)   A smell that occurs when sweat contacts bacteria on the skin.

circumcision   The removal of the foreskin covering part of the head of the penis. May be done for religious or medical reasons.

contraception   Various methods used to prevent pregnancy.

ejaculation   When semen comes out of the end of the penis.

erection   The enlargement and hardening of the penis during sexual excitement.

fertilisation   When a male sperm joins with a female egg.

genitals   The reproductive organs of men or women.

hormones   Chemical messengers that cause a change in the body.

penis   The male sex organ.

pregnancy   The time when a baby is growing inside a woman's body.

pubic hair   Body hair that grows around the penis or vagina.

scrotum   The sack of skin that contains a man's testicles.

semen   A mixture of sperm and fluid. The fluid allows the sperm to swim.

sex   Physical contact in which people touch each other's bodies. It includes intercourse, when a man's penis is inserted into a woman's vagina.

sperm   The male sex cell produced in the testicles. It is needed to make a baby.

testicles   Also known as balls, these are where sperm cells are made.

testosterone   The male sex hormone.

uterus   Part of a woman's body, also called the womb, where a fertilised egg grows into a baby.

vagina   The passage in a woman's body that leads from the uterus to the outside.

vocal cords   The muscles in the throat that widen during male puberty and change the sound of a boy's voice.

wet dreams   Dreams about sex which cause boys to ejaculate in their sleep.

Useful information

Avert	www.avert.org/sex-stis/puberty	Sexual health site that includes information about puberty.
BBC	http://tinyurl.com/hfoxjvj	BBC guide to your body and the changes it goes through at puberty.
Childline	0800 1111 www.childline.org.uk	Help and advice for kids and teens from a confidential counsellor.
Family Lives	0808 800 2222 www.familylives.org.uk	An advice organisation for parents and kids covering all areas of family life, including puberty.
NHS	http://tinyurl.com/z89nyoa	The NHS puberty information page, full of useful facts.
Shaving Tips for Men	http://tinyurl.com/gs7sgq4	Great how-to video about shaving for teens.

Index

First published in Great Britain in 2016 by Wayland

Copyright © Wayland, 2016

All rights reserved.

Editor: Liza Miller
Design: Collaborate Agency
Illustration: Sarah Horne, Advocate Art

ISBN: 978 0 7502 9893 3
10 9 8 7 6 5 4 3 2 1

Wayland
An imprint of
Hachette Children's Group
Part of Hodder & Stoughton
Carmelite House
50 Victoria Embankment
London EC4Y 0DZ

An Hachette UK Company
www.hachette.co.uk
www.hachettechildrens.co.uk

Printed in China

The website addresses (URLs) included in this book were valid at the time of going to press. However, it is possible that contents or addresses may have changed since the publication of this book. No responsibility for any such changes can be accepted by either the author or the Publisher.

FSC
www.fsc.org
MIX
Paper from responsible sources
FSC® C104740